# Harry's Big Wiener

Harry has a big weiner that goes
with him to the park, longer than a shark!

His weiner is so long,
that people on the street shout,

"That's one big weiner, in those pants!"
His weiner gets excited, and stands up!

Harry laughs and strolls around the park with his hairy weiner out in the open for all to enjoy.

As he walks, people want to come and stroke his weiner.

"That feels good, doesn't it?"
One lady says to his weiner.

The wiener is satisfied with
the attention it is receiving.

"I really like your weiner, maybe someday, your weiner can meet my kitty." The lady says.

Harry likes the sound of that,
hopefully they will both come that day.

Harry continues to walk with his weiner
and another person comes along,

"Your weiner is longer than any weiner I've ever seen!".

"Does it fit?" Another woman asked,

"Of course, it does! I have a doggy door
at home for it." Harry said proudly.

His weiner got so much attention.

Many people who walked by rubbed
his weiner so much, it was happy all day!

People at the park told Harry
about their weiner too!

Some of them were wrinkly and old,
small, and short, skinny, and fat!

Weiners come in all shapes and sizes.

"Can I touch your weiner?"
An old lady said to Harry.

"If it's not too big for you to handle!"
Harry said to the old lady.

The old lady laughed and gave
his weiner long and slow strokes,

"I've had a lot of experience with wieners.
I have a few at home!" The old lady said.

Harry and his weiner were tired
all day from the excitement.

He laid in bed, and rubbed
his weiner's tip of the nose.

"So many ladies liked you today!

Did you have fun?"
He asked his weiner

His weiner stood up with happiness again!

Harry continued to rub his weiner,

and think about how he would come
all the way to the park tomorrow!

Thanks For Buying This Book

Visit Our Author Page
For More Amazing Book Like This!

Selena Johnson